Laureate Series Artists
pictured from upper left hand corner, clockwise
around the square.

Dale Clevenger, Principal horn, Chicago Symphony
Jerome Bunke, Concert Soloist, Clinician
Vincent Abato, Concert Soloist, Metropolitan Opera Orch.
Julius Baker, Solo flute, N.Y. Philharmonic Orchestra
Keith Brown, Soloist, Professor of Music, Indiana Univ.
Armando Ghitalla, Principal trumpet, Boston Symphony
Jay Friedman, Principal trombone, Chicago Symphony
Harold Wright, Solo clarinet, Boston Symphony
Gerard Schwarz, Principal trumpet, N.Y. Philharmonic
Murray Panitz, Solo flute, Philadelphia Orchestra
Robert Nagel, Concert Soloist, N.Y. Brass Quintet
Mason Jones, Principal horn, Philadelphia Orchestra
Stanley Drucker, Solo clarinet, N.Y. Philharmonic Orch.
Donald Peck, Solo flute, Chicago Symphony Orch.
Paul Brodie, Concert Soloist, Clinician
Myron Bloom, Principal horn, Cleveland Symphony Orch.
Per Brevig, Principal trombone, Metropolitan Opera Orch.

COMMENTARY BY DORIOT ANTHONY DWYER

JOSEPH HAYDN
Adagio from Symphony No. 24

The melodic structure of this piece follows the very old concept of theme and variations. In the classical period, these variations were handled as ornaments, but it is good to think of them as variations because one needs a sense of improvisation when playing them. One of the most important improvisatory characteristics is that the notes do not proceed at the same rate, although the player must stay within the framework of the tempo. The impression must be that the overall amount of time elapsing is the same as if the notes were played exactly evenly.

The cadenza in this music is my own. However, it is best for each flutist to write his/her own version. Try to stay within the framework of Haydn's harmonies, making use of melodic material which has been played previously by either the flute or the piano. You must consider a balanced length. Short movements generally have short cadenzas, in accordance with the amount of material which you develop.

One of the most important things in a piece of this great stature is to begin a phrase where you left off from the last one, even if the phrase is very different from its predecessor. Even if you change the dynamics, retain the same mood. Note that in this type of music, you cannot "show off" by drastic changes in dynamics or overdone accents.

FELIX MENDELSSOHN
Songs Without Words

The Songs Without Words encompass 48 short piano pieces published between 1830 and 1845. They are written not in the prevailing sonata form, but in the style of a song, with a singable melody and simple, uniform accompaniment. Unlike most "character" pieces of the nineteenth century, they have no contrasting middle sections.

Opus 62, No. 1

This piece, although labeled Op. 62, No. 25 in Louis Moyse's *Solos for the Flute Player,* from which this arrangement is taken, is actually the first piece of that opus. The entire piece is derived from the first two quarter notes. All that follows consists of motion toward the next two quarter notes. If you view the piece in this manner, you can easily find where to build and where to relax—in other words, how to sing the piece.

Opus 102, No. 3

The most difficult aspect of this piece is to blend your part with the piano. The triplet figures must seem continuous, even when alternating between the flute and piano, as in bars 23 and 24. Both intonation and articulation must be exactly together in the unison passage between bars 32 and 39.

The tempo which I take on this record is just one of many possibilities. Sometimes you can give a feeling of fleetness by playing slightly slower than your top speed. Keep up your humor as you keep up your coordination with the piano.

JACOB AVSCHALOMOFF
Disconsolate Muse

This piece is a very good study for much of the Romantic literature for the flute, which unfortunately exists mainly in orchestral parts. Although his father was Russian and his mother American, Mr. Avschalomoff spent his childhood in China. There are many traces of Chinese music in this piece, though I would characterize the style as basically Russian Romantic. There are even some operatic style passages for the flute. I hope that as you play this piece, you will enjoy executing all of these various styles.

The key to this piece is working it out rhythmically, resolving the differences between the flute and piano parts in order to achieve effective ensemble. Even where you do coincide rhythmically with the accompaniment, try not to sound too mechanical. The grace notes should be very short, with very little vibrato on the following notes to give a slightly nasal sound. These figures reminded the composer of Chinese merchants in the streets. Some, however, remind me of *La Bohème* and *Madame Butterfly,* and so you may hear some of the grace note figures in the Chinese manner, and some with vibrato after them in a more operatic manner. Thus you cannot follow these instructions too literally; you must evolve your own style of performance.

JEAN MARTINON
Sonatine

Each of the three sections of the *Sonatine* should have a distinctive character. Be sure that the first section is not too slow. To avoid this, I suggest that you think in units of a measure, rather than of each beat. This will keep the motion from becoming too ponderous.

The second section, which is marked *piano,* must have a very different tone quality from the first. The section gets more animated as it goes along, but remember to save some of that energy for the final section. Be sure to observe the diminuendos on the slurs in measures 65 and 66. Mr. Martinon is adamant about the observation of dynamics, especially the diminuendos in the ascending scales.

In the last section, make use of the large intervals in the first bar to achieve a contrast with the preceding section. In the repetition of the Presto, you are instructed to jump to the coda from measure 31. Be sure to make a crescendo in the second bar of the coda (measure 73) to make the coda seem convincing. The two sixteenths-eighth note figures in measures 78 to 81 are well marked, and should be closely imitated by the flute from measures 98 to 101. It is the propulsion of this rhythm which drives the piece triumphantly to the end. There is no ritard in the final measures!

Doriot Anthony Dwyer

ADAGIO
from Symphony No. 24

Joseph Haydn

BAND 1   6 taps (1 measure) precede music.

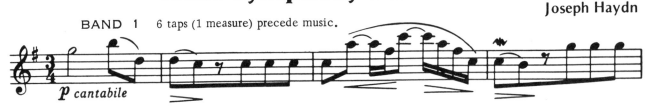

3331

Cadenza ad libitum

3331

SONG WITHOUT WORDS
Op. 62, No.1

BAND 2   2 taps (1/2 measure) precede music.

Felix Mendelssohn

3331

SONG WITHOUT WORDS
Op. 102, No. 3

BAND 3 (Practice Tempo)

BAND 4 4 taps (2 measures) precede music.

Felix Mendelssohn

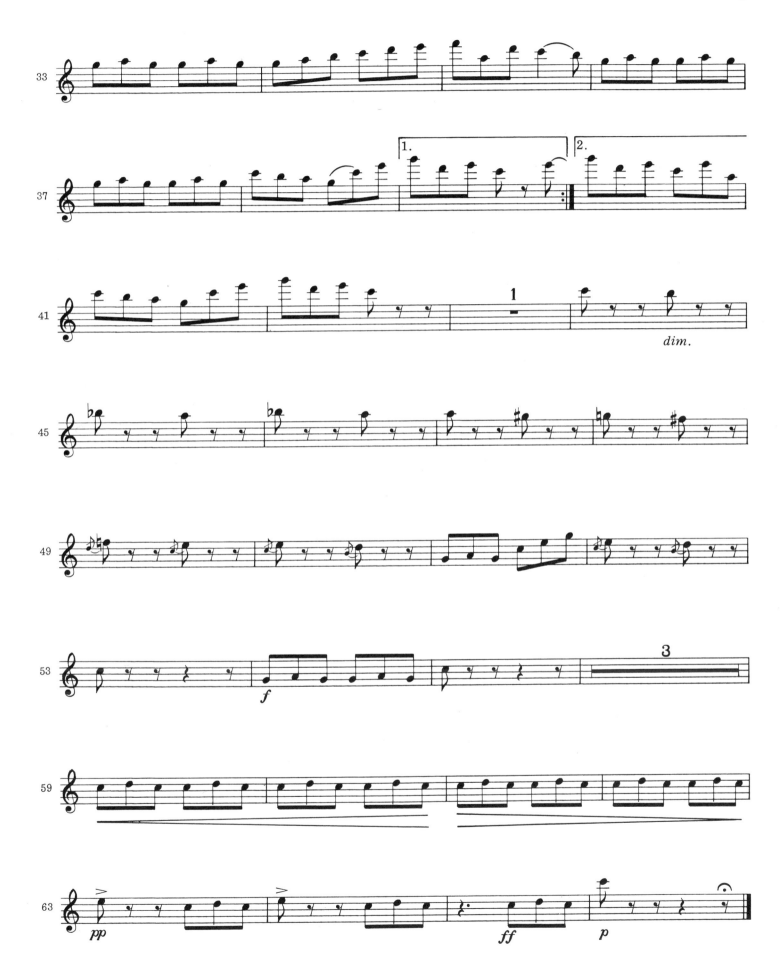

DISCONSOLATE MUSE

BAND 5   4 taps (2 measures) precede music.

Jacob Avschalomoff

Laureate Series Contest Solos

A new series from MMO featuring the choicest repertoire for the instrument as performed by the foremost players in the land and then by YOU. Graded for easy choice. Each album comes with completely annotated solo part, cues and suggestions for performance.

MMO 8001   **Beginning Level**

Gretchaninoff — First Waltz
Hopkins — Wanton Waltz
   and Flirtatious Fancy
Lewallen — Poeme Petite

Lully — Dances for the King
Schubert — Three Themes

MURRAY PANITZ — Soloist   HARRIETT WINGREEN — Pianist

MMO 8002   **Beginning Level**

Gossec — Gavotte
Hindemith — Echo
Kuhlau — Menuett
Lewallen — Andantino

Marpurg — Rondo
Sumerlin — Serenade
Tailleferre — Pastorale

DONALD PECK — Soloist   JUDITH OLSON — Pianist

MMO 8003   **Intermediate Level**

Handel — Sonata No. 5 in F
Pessard — Andalouse

Telemann — Sonata No. 7 in C Minor
   (1st mvt.)

JULIUS BAKER — Soloist   MARTHA REARICK — Pianist

MMO 8004   **Intermediate Level**

Bach — Suite in B Minor
   (Polonaise & Badinerie)
Baksa — Aria da Capo

Marcello — Sonata in F
Widor — Scherzo

DONALD PECK — Soloist   JUDITH OLSON — Pianist

MMO 8005   **Advanced Level**

Bach — Sonata No. 2 in E♭
   (1st & 2nd mvts)
Hindemith — Sonata (1st mvt.)

Mozart — Concerto No. 2 in D,
   K. 314 (1st mvt.)

MURRAY PANITZ — Soloist   HARRIET WINGREEN — Pianist

MMO 8006   **Advanced Level**

Bach — Sonata No. 7 in G Minor
   (1st mvt.)
Faure — Fantasie, Op. 79

Mozart — Concerto No. 1 in G,
   K 313, (1st mvt.)

JULIUS BAKER — Soloist   MARTHA REARICK — Pianist

MMO 8007   **Intermediate Level**

Andersen — Scherzino
Gluck — Minuet and Dance of the
   Blessed Spirits
Handel — Sonata No. 3 in G
   (1st & 2nd mvts.)

Lane — Sonata (1st mvt.)
Mozart — Andante in C, K 315

DONALD PECK — Soloist   JUDITH OLSON — Pianist

MMO 8008   **Advanced Level**

Handel — Sonata No. 2 in G Minor
   (1st & 4th mvts.)
Henze — Sonatine (1st mvt.)

Quantz — Concerto in G (1st mvt.)
Telemann — Suite in A Minor
   ('Les Plaisirs')

MURRAY PANITZ — Soloist   HARRIET WINGREEN — Pianist

MMO 8009   **Advanced Level**

Bach — Arioso
Faure — Sicilienne
Godard — Idylle

Platti — Sonata No. 2 in G
   (3rd & 4th mvts.)

JULIUS BAKER — Soloist   MARTHA REARICK — Pianist

SONATINE

Jean Martinon

(*) *Omet si nécessaire.*

16

3331

Music Minus One 50 Executive Blvd. Elmsford, New York 10523-1325
phone: 914 592 1188   fax: 1-914- 592 3575 Email: music@mmogroup.com Printed in Canada.